MW00378122

Forever Grateful To You: